BY JOSEPH BRODSKY

Elegy for John Donne and Other Poems
Selected Poems
A Part of Speech
Less Than One
To Urania
Marbles
Watermark

WATERMARK

WATERMARK

JOSEPH BRODSKY

Farrar, Straus & Giroux

New York

Library of Congress Cataloging-in-Publication Data

Brodsky, Joseph

Watermark / Joseph Brodsky. — 1st ed.

1. Venice (Italy)—Description—1981–   2. Brodsky, Joseph. 1940–
—Journeys—Italy—Venice.   I. Title.

PG3479.4.R64W3   1992   818'.5403—dc20   [B]   91-45351   CIP

To Robert Morgan

WATERMARK

many moons ago the dollar was 870 lire and I was thirty-two. The globe, too, was lighter by two billion souls, and the bar at the *stazione* where I'd arrived on that cold December night was empty. I was standing there waiting for the only person I knew in that city to meet me. She was quite late.

Every traveler knows this fix: this mixture of fatigue and apprehension. It's the time of staring down clock faces and timetables, of scrutinizing varicose marble under your feet, of inhaling ammonia and that dull smell elicited on cold winter nights by locomotives' cast iron. I did all this.

Save for the yawning bartender and immobile Buddha-like *matrona* at the cash register, there was no one in sight. However, we were of no use to each other: my sole currency in their language, the term "espresso," was already spent; I'd used it twice. I'd also bought from them my first pack ever of what in years to come was to stand for "*Merde Statale*," "*Movimento Sociale*," and "*Morte Sicura*": my first pack of MS. So I lifted my bags and stepped outside.

In the unlikely event that someone's eye followed my white London Fog and dark brown Borsalino, they should have cut a familiar silhouette. The night itself, to be sure, would have had no difficulty absorbing it. Mimicry, I believe, is high on the list of every traveler, and the Italy I had in mind at the moment was a fusion of black-and-white movies of the fifties and the equally monochrome medium of my métier. Winter thus was my season; the only thing I lacked, I thought, to look like a local rake or *carbonaro* was a scarf. Other than that, I felt inconspicuous and fit to merge into the background or fill the frame of a low-budget whodunit or, more likely, melodrama.

t was a windy night, and before my retina registered anything, I was smitten by a feeling of utter happiness: my nostrils were hit by what to me has always been its synonym, the smell of freezing seaweed. For some people, it's freshly cut grass or hay; for others, Christmas scents of conifer needles and tangerines. For me, it's freezing seaweed—partly because of onomatopoeic aspects of the very conjunction (in Russian, seaweed is a wonderful *vodorosli*), partly due to a slight incongruity and a hidden underwater drama in this notion. One recognizes oneself in certain elements; by the time I was taking this smell in on the steps of the *stazione*, hidden

dramas and incongruities long since had become my forte.

No doubt the attraction toward that smell should have been attributed to a childhood spent by the Baltic, the home of that meandering siren from the Montale poem. And yet I had my doubts about this attribution. For one thing, that childhood wasn't all that happy (a childhood seldom is, being, rather, a school of self-disgust and insecurity); and as for the Baltic, you had indeed to be an eel to escape my part of it. At any rate, as a subject for nostalgia this childhood hardly qualified. The source of that attraction, I'd always felt, lay elsewhere, beyond the confines of biography, beyond one's genetic makeup—somewhere in one's hypothalamus, which stores our chordate ancestors' impressions of their native realm of—for example—the very ichthus that caused this civilization. Whether that ichthus was a happy one is another matter.

smell is, after all, a violation of oxygen balance, an invasion into it of other elements—methane? carbon? sulphur? nitrogen? Depending on that invasion's intensity, you get a scent, a smell, a stench. It is a molecular affair, and happiness, I suppose, is the moment of spotting the elements of your own composition being free. There were quite a number of them out there, in a state of total freedom, and I felt I'd stepped into my own self-portrait in the cold air.

The backdrop was all in dark silhouettes of church cupolas and rooftops; a bridge arching over a body of water's black curve, both ends of which were clipped off by infinity. At night, infinity in foreign realms arrives with the last lamppost, and here it was twenty meters away. It was very quiet. A few dimly lit boats now and then prowled about, disturbing with their propellers the reflection of a large neon CIN-ZANO trying to settle on the black oilcloth of the water's surface. Long before it succeeded, the silence would be restored.

t all felt like arriving in the provinces, in some unknown, insignificant spot—possibly one's own birthplace—after years of absence. In no small degree did this sensation owe to my own anonymity, to the incongruity of a lone figure on the steps of the *stazione*: an easy target for oblivion. Also, it was a winter night. And I remembered the opening line of one of Umberto Saba's poems that I'd translated long before, in a previous incarnation, into Russian: "In the depths of the wild Adriatic . . ." In the depths, I thought, in the boondocks, in a lost corner of the wild Adriatic . . . Had I simply turned around, I'd have seen the *stazione* in all its rectangular splendor of neon and urbanity, seen block letters saying VENEZIA. Yet I didn't. The sky was full of winter stars, the way it often is in the

provinces. At any point, it seemed, a dog could bark in the distance, or else you might hear a rooster. With my eyes shut I beheld a tuft of freezing seaweed splayed against a wet, perhaps ice-glazed rock somewhere in the universe, oblivious to its location. I was that rock, and my left palm was that splayed tuft of seaweed. Presently a large, flat boat, something of a cross between a sardine can and a sandwich, emerged out of nowhere and with a thud nudged the *stazione*'s landing. A handful of people pushed ashore and raced past me up the stairs into the terminal. Then I saw the only person I knew in that city; the sight was fabulous.

 had seen it for the first time several years before, in that same previous incarnation: in Russia. The sight had come there in the guise of a Slavicist, a Mayakovsky scholar, to be precise. That nearly disqualified

the sight as a subject of interest in the eyes of the coterie to which I belonged. That it didn't was the measure of her visual properties. Five foot ten, fine-boned, long-legged, narrow-faced, with chestnut hair and hazel, almond-shaped eyes, with passable Russian on those wonderfully shaped lips and a blinding smile on the same, superbly dressed in paper-light suede and matching silks, redolent of mes-merizing, unknown to us, perfume, the sight was easily the most elegant female ever to set a mind-boggling foot in our midst. She was the kind that keeps married men's dreams wet. Besides, she was a Veneziana.

So we gave short shrift to her membership in the Italian CP and her attendant sentiment toward our avant-garde simpletons of the thir-ties, attributing both to Western frivolity. Had she been even an avowed Fascist, I think we would have lusted after her no less. She was positively stunning, and when subsequently she'd fallen for the worst possible dimwit on the periphery of our circle, some highly paid dolt of Armenian extraction, the common response was amazement and anger rather than jealousy or manly regret. Of course, come to think of it, one shouldn't get angry over a piece of fine lace soiled by some strong ethnic juices. Yet we did. For it was more than a letdown: it was a betrayal of the fabric.

In those days we associated style with substance, beauty with intelligence. After all, we were a bookish crowd, and at a certain age, if you believe in literature, you think everyone shares or should share your conviction and taste. So if one looks elegant, one is one of us. Innocent of the world outside, of the West in particular, we didn't know yet that style could be purchased wholesale, that beauty could be just a commodity. So we regarded the sight as the physical extension and embodiment of our ideals and principles, and what she wore, transparent things included, belonged to civilization.

So strong was that association, and so pretty was the sight, that even now, years later, belonging to a different age and, as it were, to a different country, I began to slip unwittingly into the old mode. The first thing I asked her as I stood pressed to her nutria coat on the deck of the overcrowded vaporetto was her opinion of Montale's *Motets*, recently published. The familiar flash of her pearls, thirty-two strong, echoed by the sparkle on the rim of her hazel pupil and promoted to the scattered silver of the Milky Way overhead, was all I got in response, but that was a lot. To ask, in the heart of civilization, about its latest was perhaps a tautology. Perhaps I was simply being impolite, as the author wasn't a local.

he boat's slow progress through the night was like the passage of a coherent thought through the subconscious. On both sides, knee-deep in pitch-black water, stood the enormous carved chests of dark pa-

lazzi filled with unfathomable treasures—most likely gold, judging from the low-intensity yellow electric glow emerging now and then from cracks in the shutters. The overall feeling was mythological, cyclopic, to be precise: I'd entered that infinity I beheld on the steps of the *stazione* and now was moving among its inhabitants, along the bevy of dormant cyclopses reclining in black water, now and then raising and lowering an eyelid.

The nutria-clad sight next to me began explaining in a somewhat hushed voice that she was taking me to my hotel, where she had reserved a room, that perhaps we'd meet tomorrow or the day after, that she'd like to introduce me to her husband and her sister. I liked the hush in her voice, though it fit the night more than the message, and replied in the same conspiratorial tones that it's always a pleasure to meet potential relatives. That was a bit strong for the moment, but she laughed, in the same muffled way, putting a hand in a brown leather glove to her lips. The passengers around us, mostly dark-haired, whose number was responsible for our proximity, were immobile and equally subdued in their occasional remarks to one another, as though the content of their exchanges was also of an intimate nature. Then the sky was momentarily obscured by the huge marble parenthesis of a bridge, and suddenly everything was flooded with light. "Rialto," she said in her normal voice.

here is something primordial about traveling on water, even for short distances. You are informed that you are not supposed to be there not so much by your eyes, ears, nose, palate, or palm as by your feet, which feel odd acting as an organ of sense. Water unsettles the principle of horizontality, especially at night, when its surface resembles pavement. No matter how solid its substitute

—the deck—under your feet, on water you are somewhat more alert than ashore, your faculties are more poised. On water, for instance, you never get absentminded the way you do in the street: your legs keep you and your wits in constant check, as if you were some kind of compass. Well, perhaps what sharpens your wits while traveling on water is indeed a distant, roundabout echo of the good old chordates. At any rate, your sense of the other on water gets keener, as though heightened by a common as well as a mutual danger. The loss of direction is a psychological category as much as it is a navigational one. Be that as it may, for the next ten minutes, although we were moving in the same direction, I saw the arrow of the only person I knew in that city and mine diverge by at least 45 degrees. Most likely because this part of the Canal Grande was better lit.

We disembarked at the Accademia landing, prey to firm topography and the corresponding moral code. After a short meander through narrow lanes, I was deposited in the lobby of a somewhat cloistered *pensione*, kissed on the cheek—more in the capacity of the Minotaur, I felt, than the valiant hero—and wished good night. Then my Ariadne vanished, leaving behind a fragrant thread of her expensive (was it Shalimar?) perfume, which quickly dissipated in the musty atmosphere of a *pensione* otherwise suffused with the faint but ubiquitous odor of pee. I stared for a while at the furniture. Then I hit the sack.

hat's how I found myself for the first time in this city. As it turned out, there was nothing particularly auspicious or ominous about this arrival of mine. If that night portended anything at all, it was that I'd never possess this city; but then I never had any such aspiration. As a beginning, I think this episode

will do, although as far as the-only-person-I-knew-in-this-city was concerned, it rather marked the end of our acquaintance. I saw her two or three times subsequently during that stay in Venice; and indeed I was introduced to her sister and to her husband. The former turned out to be a lovely woman: as tall and slender as my Ariadne and perhaps even brighter, but more melancholy and, for all I could tell, even more married. The latter, whose appearance completely escapes my memory for reasons of redundancy, was a scumbag of an architect, of that ghastly post-war persuasion that has done more harm to the European skyline than any Luftwaffe. In Venice, he defiled a couple of wonderful *campi* with his edifices, one of which was naturally a bank, since this sort of human animal loves a bank with absolutely narcissistic fervor, with the longing of an effect for its cause. For that "structure" (as they called it in those days) alone, I thought, he should be cuckolded. But since, like his wife, he, too, seemed to be a member of the CP, the job, I concluded, was best left to a comrade.

Fastidiousness was one part of it; the other part was that when, somewhat later, I called the-only-person-I-knew-in-that-city from the depths of my labyrinth one blue evening, the architect, perhaps sensing in my broken Italian something untoward, cut the thread. So now it really was up to our red Armenian brethren.

ubsequently, I was told, she divorced the man and married a U.S. Air Force pilot, who turned out to be the nephew of the mayor of a small town in the great state of Michigan, where I once dwelt. Small world, and the longer you live, no man or woman makes it larger. So were I looking for consolation, I could derive it from the thought that we now are both treading the same ground—

of a different continent. This sounds, of course, like Statius talking to Virgil, but then it's only proper for the likes of me to regard America as a kind of Purgatorio—not to mention Dante himself suggesting as much. The only difference is that her heaven is far better settled than mine. Hence my forays into my version of Paradise, which she inaugurated so graciously. At any rate, for the last seventeen years I've been returning to this city, or recurring in it, with the frequency of a bad dream.

With two or three exceptions, due to heart attacks and related emergencies, mine or someone else's, every Christmas or shortly before I'd emerge from a train/plane/boat/bus and drag my bags heavy with books and typewriters to the threshold of this or that hotel, of this or that apartment. The latter would normally be courtesy of the one or two friends I'd managed to develop here in the wake of the sight's dimming. Later, I'll try to account for my timing (though such a project is tautological to the point of reversal). For the moment, I'd like to assert that, Northerner though I am, my notion of Eden hinges on neither weather nor temperature. For that matter, I'd just as soon discard its dwellers, and eternity as well. At the risk of being charged with depravity, I confess that this notion is purely visual, has more to do with Claude than the creed, and exists only in approximations. As these go, this city is the closest. Since I'm not entitled to make a true comparison, I can permit myself to be restrictive.

I say this here and now to save the reader disillusionment. I am not a moral man (though I try to keep my conscience in balance) or a sage; I am neither an aesthete nor a philosopher. I am but a nervous man, by circumstance and by my own deeds; but I am observant. As my beloved Akutagawa Ryunosuke once said, I have no principles; all I've got is nerves. What follows, therefore, has to do with the eye rather than with convictions, including those as to how to run a narrative. One's eye precedes one's pen, and I resolve not to let my pen lie about its position. Having risked the charge of depravity, I won't wince at that of superficiality either. Surfaces—which is what the eye registers first—are often more telling than their contents, which are provisional by definition, except, of course, in the afterlife. Scanning this city's face for seventeen winters, I should by now be capable of pulling a credible Poussin-like job: of painting this place's likeness, if not at four seasons, then at four times of day.

That's my ambition. If I get sidetracked, it is because being sidetracked is literally a matter of course here and echoes water. What lies ahead, in other words, may amount not to a story but to the flow of muddy water "at the wrong time of year." At times it looks blue, at times gray or brown; invariably it is cold and not potable. The reason I am engaged in straining it is that it contains reflections, among them my own.

nanimate by nature, hotel room mirrors are even further dulled by having seen so many. What they return to you is not your identity but your anonymity, especially in this city. For here yourself is the last thing you care to see. On my first sojourns I often felt surprised, catching my own frame, dressed or naked, in the open wardrobe; after a while I began to wonder about this place's edenic or afterlife-like effects upon one's self-awareness. Somewhere along the line, I even developed a theory of excessive redundancy, of the mirror absorbing the body absorbing the city. The net result is, obviously, mutual negation. A reflection cannot possibly care for a reflection. The city is narcissistic enough to turn your mind into an amalgam, unburdening it of its depths. With their similar effect on your purse, hotels and *pensiones* therefore feel very congenial. After a two-week stay—even at off-season rates—you become both broke and self-

less, like a Buddhist monk. At a certain age and in a certain line of work, selflessness is welcome, not to say imperative.

Nowadays all of this is, of course, out of the question, since the clever devils shut down two-thirds of the small places in winter; the remaining third keep year round those summer rates that make you wince. If you're lucky, you may find an apartment, which, naturally, comes with the owner's personal taste in paintings, chairs, curtains, with a vague sense of illegality to your face in his bathroom mirror —in short, with precisely what you wanted to shed: yourself. Still, winter is an abstract season: it is low on colors, even in Italy, and big on the imperatives of cold and brief daylight. These things train your eye on the outside with an intensity greater than that of the electric bulb availing you of your own features in the evening. If this season doesn't necessarily quell your nerves, it still subordinates them to your instincts; beauty at low temperatures *is* beauty.

nyhow, I would never come here in summer, not even at gunpoint. I take heat very poorly; the unmitigated emissions of hydrocarbons and armpits still worse. The shorts-clad herds, especially those neighing in German, also get on my nerves, because of the inferiority of their—anyone's—anatomy against that of the columns, pilasters, and statues; because of what their mobility—and all that fuels it—projects versus marble stasis. I guess I am one of those who prefer choice to flux, and stone is always a choice. No matter how well endowed, in this city one's body, in my view, should be obscured by cloth, if only because it moves. Clothes are perhaps our only approximation of the choice made by marble.

This is, I suppose, an extreme view, but I am a Northerner. In the abstract season life seems more real than at any other, even in the Adriatic, because in winter everything is harder, more stark. Or else take this as propaganda for Venetian boutiques, which do extremely brisk business in low temperatures. In part, of course, this is so because in winter one needs more clothes just to stay warm, not to mention the atavistic urge to shed one's pelt. Yet no traveler comes here without a spare sweater, jacket, skirt, shirt, slacks, or blouse, since Venice is the sort of city where both the stranger and the native know in advance that one will be on display.

No, bipeds go ape about shopping and dressing up in Venice for reasons not exactly practical; they do so because the city, as it were, challenges them. We all harbor all sorts of misgivings about the flaws in our appearance, anatomy, about the imperfection of our very features. What one sees in this city at every step, turn, perspective, and dead end worsens one's complexes and insecurities. That's why one—a woman especially, but a man also— hits the stores as soon as one arrives here, and with a vengeance. The surrounding beauty is such that one instantly conceives of an incoherent animal desire to match it, to be on a par. This has nothing to do with vanity or with the natural surplus of mirrors here, the main one being the very water. It is simply that the city offers bipeds a notion of visual superiority absent in their natural lairs, in their habitual surroundings. That's why furs fly here, as do suede, silk, linen, wool, and every other kind of fabric. Upon returning home, folks stare in wonderment at what they've acquired, knowing full well that there is no place in their native realm to flaunt these acquisitions without scandalizing the natives. You must keep those things fading and withering in your wardrobe, or else give them to your younger relations. Or else, there are friends. I, for one, remember buying several items here—on credit, obviously—that I had no stomach or nerve to utilize later. Among them were two raincoats, one mustard green and the other a gentle shade of khaki. Later they were to grace the shoulders of the world's best ballet dancer and the best poet of the language I write this in—distinct though both these gentlemen are from me in size and age. It's the local vistas and perspectives that do it, for in this city a man is more a silhouette than his unique features, and a silhouette can be improved. It's also the marble lace, inlays, capitals, cornices, reliefs, and moldings, inhabited and uninhabited niches, saints, ain'ts, maidens, angels, cherubs, caryatids, pediments, balconies with their ample kicked-up calves, and windows themselves, Gothic or Moorish, that turn you vain. For this is the city of the eye; your other faculties play a faint second fiddle. The way the hues and rhythms of the local façades try to smooth the waves' ever-changing colors and patterns alone may send you to grab a fancy scarf, tie, or whatnot; it glues even an inveterate bachelor to a window flooded with its motley flaunted dresses, not to mention patent-leather shoes and suede boots scattered like all sorts of boats upon the *laguna*. Somehow your eye suspects that all these things are cut from the same cloth as the vistas outside and ignores the evidence of labels. And in the final analysis, the eye is not so wrong, if only because the common purpose of everything here is to be *seen*. In an analysis even more final, this city is a real triumph of the chordate, because the eye, our only raw, fishlike internal organ, indeed swims here: it darts, flaps, oscillates, dives, rolls up. Its exposed jelly dwells with atavistic joy on reflected palazzi, spiky heels, gondolas, etc., recognizing in the agency that brought them to the existential surface none other than itself.

n winter you wake up in this city, especially on Sundays, to the chiming of its innumerable bells, as though behind your gauze curtains a gigantic china teaset were vibrating on a silver tray in the pearl-gray sky. You fling the window open and the room is

instantly flooded with this outer, peal-laden haze, which is part damp oxygen, part coffee and prayers. No matter what sort of pills, and how many, you've got to swallow this morning, you feel it's not over for you yet. No matter, by the same token, how autonomous you are, how much you've been betrayed, how thorough and dispiriting is your self-knowledge, you assume there is still hope for you, or at least a future. (Hope, said Francis Bacon, is a good breakfast but a bad supper.) This optimism derives from the haze, from the prayer part of it, especially if it is time for breakfast. On days like this, the city indeed acquires a porcelain aspect, what with all its zinc-covered cupolas resembling teapots or up-turned cups, and the tilted profile of campaniles clinking like abandoned spoons and melting in the sky. Not to mention the seagulls and pigeons, now sharpening into focus, now melting into air. I should say that, good though this place is for honeymoons, I've often thought it should be tried for divorces also—

both in progress and already accomplished. There is no better backdrop for rapture to fade into; whether right or wrong, no egoist can star for long in this porcelain setting by crystal water, for it steals the show. I am aware, of course, of the disastrous consequence the above suggestions may have for hotel rates here, even in winter. Still, people love their melodrama more than architecture, and I don't feel threatened. It is surprising that beauty is valued less than psychology, but so long as such is the case, I'll be able to afford this city—which means till the end of my days, and which ushers in the generous notion of the future.

ne is what one looks at—well, at least partially. The medieval belief that a pregnant woman wishing her child to be beautiful must look at beautiful objects is not so naïve given the quality of dreams one dreams in this city. Nights here are low on night-

mares—judging of course by literary sources (especially since nightmares are such sources' main fare). Wherever he goes, a sick man, for example—a cardiac cripple particularly—is bound to wake up now and then at three o'clock in the morning in a state of sheer terror, thinking he's going. Yet nothing of the sort, I must report, ever happened to me here; though as I write this, I keep my fingers and toes crossed.

There are better ways, no doubt, to manipulate dreams, and no doubt a good case can be made for it being best done gastronomically. Yet by Italian standards, the local diet is not exceptional enough to account for this city's concentration of indeed dreamlike beauty in its façades alone. For in dreams, as the poet said, begin responsibilities. In any case, some of the blueprints—an apt term in this city!—certainly sprang from that source, as there is nothing else one can trace them to in reality.

Should a poet mean to say simply, "In bed," that would hold, too. Architecture is surely the least carnal of Muses, since the rectangular principle of a building, of its façade in particular, militates—and often sharply so—against your analyst's interpretation of its cloud- or wave-like—rather than feminine!—cornices, loggias, and whatnot. A blueprint, in short, is always more lucid than its analysis. Yet many a *frontone* here reminds you precisely of a headboard looming above its habitually unmade bed, be it morning or evening. They are far more absorbing, these headboards, than those beds' possible contents, than the anatomy of your beloved, whose only advantage here could be agility or warmth.

If there is anything erotic to those blueprints' marble consequences, it is the sensation caused by the eye trained on any of them—the sensation similar to that of the fingertips touching for the first time your beloved's breast or, better yet, shoulder. It is the telescopic sensation of coming in contact with the cellular infinity of another body's existence—a sensation

known as tenderness and proportionate perhaps only to the number of cells that body
contains. (Everyone would understand this,
save Freudians, or Muslims believing in the
veil. But then again, that may explain why
among Muslims there are so many astrono-
mers. Besides, the veil is a great social planning device, since it ensures every female a
man regardless of her appearance. Worst
come to worst, it guarantees that the first-
night shock is at least mutual. Still, for all
the Oriental motifs in Venetian architecture, Muslims in this city are the most infre-
quent visitors.) In any case, whichever comes
first—reality or dream—one's notion of afterlife in this city appears to be well taken care
of by its clearly paradisaical visual texture.
Sickness alone, no matter how grave it may
be, won't avail you here of an infernal vision.
You'd need an extraordinary neurosis, or a
comparable accumulation of sins, or both, to
fall prey to nightmares on these premises.

That's possible, of course, but not too frequent. For the mild cases of either, a sojourn here is the best therapy, and that's what tourism, locally, is all about. One sleeps tight in this city, since one's feet get too tired quelling a worked-up psyche or guilty conscience alike.

erhaps the best proof of the Almighty's existence is that we never know when we are to die. In other words, had life been a solely human affair, one would be issued at birth with a term, or a sentence, stating precisely the duration of one's presence here: the way it is done in prison camps. That this doesn't happen suggests that the affair is not entirely human; that something we've got no idea or control of interferes. That there is an agency which is not subject to our chronology or, for that matter, our sense of virtue. Hence

all these attempts to foretell or figure out one's future, hence one's reliance on physicians and gypsies, which intensifies once we are ill or in trouble, and which is but an attempt at domesticating—or demonizing—the divine. The same applies to our sentiment for beauty, natural and man-made alike, since the infinite can be appreciated only by the finite. Except for grace, the reasons for reciprocity would be unfathomable—unless one truly seeks a benevolent explanation of why they charge you so much for everything in this city.

y profession, or rather by the cumulative effect of what I've been doing over the years, I am a writer; by trade, however, I am an academic, a teacher. The winter break at my school is five weeks long, and that's what in part explains the timing of my pilgrimages here—but only in part. What Paradise and vacation have in common is that you have to pay for both, and the coin is your previous life. Fittingly then, my romance with this city—with this city in this particular season—started long ago: long before I developed marketable skills, long before I could afford my passion.

Sometime in 1966—I was twenty-six then —a friend lent me three short novels by a French writer, Henri de Régnier, translated into Russian by the wonderful Russian poet Mikhail Kuzmin. All I knew about Régnier at that time was that he was one of the last Parnassians, a good poet but no great shakes. All I knew by heart of Kuzmin was a handful of his *Alexandrian Songs* and *Clay Pigeons*—plus his reputation as a great aesthete, devout Orthodox, and avowed homosexual—I think, in that order.

By the time I'd got those novels, both their author and their translator were long dead. The books, too, were quite moribund: paperbacks, published in the late thirties, with no bindings to speak of, disintegrating in your palm. I remember neither their titles nor their publisher; in fact, I am quite vague on their respective plots also. Somehow I am under the impression that one of them was called *Provincial Entertainments*, but I am not sure. I could double-check, of course, but then the friend who lent them to me died a year ago; and I won't.

They were a cross between picaresque and detective novels, and at least one of them, the one I call in my mind *Provincial Entertainments*, was set in Venice in winter. Its atmosphere was twilit and dangerous, its topography aggravated with mirrors; the main events were taking place on the other side of the amalgam, within some abandoned palazzo. Like many books of the twenties, it was fairly short—some two hundred pages, no more—and its pace was brisk. The subject was the usual: love and betrayal. The main thing: the book was written in short, page or page-and-a-half chapters. From their pace came the sense of damp, cold, narrow streets through which one hurries in the evening in a state of growing apprehension, turning left, turning right. For somebody with my birthplace, the city emerging from these pages was easily recognizable and felt like Petersburg's extension into a better history, not to mention latitude. However, what mattered for me most at the impressionable stage at which I came across this novel was that it taught me the most crucial lesson in composition; namely, that what makes a narrative good is not the story itself but what follows what. Unwittingly, I came to associate this principle with Venice. If the reader now suffers, that's why.

hen one day another friend, who is still alive, brought me a disheveled issue of *Life* magazine with a stunning color photo of San Marco covered with snow. Then a bit later a girl whom I was courting at the

time made me a birthday present of an accordion set of sepia postcards her grandmother had brought from a pre-revolutionary honeymoon in Venice, and I pored over it with my magnifying glass. Then my mother produced from God knows where a small square piece of cheap tapestry, a rag really, depicting the Palazzo Ducale, and it covered the bolster on my Turkish sofa—thus contracting the history of the republic under my frame. And throw into the bargain a little copper gondola brought by my father from his tour of duty in China, which my parents kept on their dressing table, filling it with loose buttons, needles, postage stamps, and—increasingly—pills and ampoules. Then the friend who gave me Régnier's novels and who died a year ago took me to a semiofficial screening of the smuggled, and for that reason black-and-white, copy of Visconti's *Death in Venice* with Dirk Bogarde. Alas, the movie wasn't much to speak of; besides, I never liked the novel much, either.

Still, the long opening sequence with Mr. Bogarde in a deck chair aboard a steamer made me forget about the interfering credits and regret that I was not mortally ill; even today I am still capable of feeling that regret.

Then came the *Veneziana*. I began to feel that this city somehow was barging into focus, tottering on the verge of the three-dimensional. It was black-and-white, as befits something emerging from literature, or winter; aristocratic, darkish, cold, dimly lit, with twangs of Vivaldi and Cherubini in the background, with Bellini/Tiepolo/Titian-draped female bodies for clouds. And I vowed to myself that should I ever get out of my empire, should this eel ever escape the Baltic, the first thing I would do would be to come to Venice, rent a room on the ground floor of some palazzo so that the waves raised by passing boats would splash against my window, write a couple of elegies while extinguishing my cigarettes on the damp stony floor, cough and drink, and, when the money got short, instead of boarding a train, buy myself a little Browning and blow my brains out on the spot, unable to die in Venice of natural causes.

perfectly decadent dream, of course; but at the age of twenty-eight everyone who's got some brains is a touch decadent. Besides, neither part of that project was feasible. So when at the age of thirty-two I all of a sudden found myself in the bowels of a different continent, in the middle of America, I used my first university salary to enact the better part of that dream and bought a round-trip ticket, Detroit–Milano–Detroit. The plane was jammed with Italians employed by Ford and Chrysler and going home for Christmas. When the duty-free opened mid-flight, all of them rushed to the plane's rear, and for a moment I had a vision of a good old 707 flying

over the Atlantic crucifix-like: wings out-stretched, tail down. Then there was the train ride with the only person I knew in the city at its end. The end was cold, damp, black-and-white. The city came into focus. "And the earth was without form, and void; and darkness was upon the face of the deep. And the Spirit of God moved upon the face of the waters," to quote an author who visited here before. Then there was that next morning. It was Sunday, and all the bells were chiming.

always adhered to the idea that God is time, or at least that His spirit is. Perhaps this idea was even of my own manufacture, but now I don't remember. In any case, I always thought that if the Spirit of God moved upon the face of the water, the water was bound to reflect it. Hence my sentiment for water, for its folds, wrinkles, and ripples,

and—as I am a Northerner—for its grayness. I simply think that water is the image of time, and every New Year's Eve, in somewhat pagan fashion, I try to find myself near water, preferably near a sea or an ocean, to watch the emergence of a new helping, a new cupful of time from it. I am not looking for a naked maiden riding on a shell; I am looking for either a cloud or the crest of a wave hitting the shore at midnight. That, to me, is time coming out of water, and I stare at the lace-like pattern it puts on the shore, not with a gypsy-like knowing, but with tenderness and with gratitude.

This is the way, and in my case the why, I set my eyes on this city. There is nothing Freudian to this fantasy, or specifically chordate, although some evolutionary—if not plainly atavistic—or autobiographical connection could no doubt be established between the pattern a wave leaves upon the sand and its scrutiny by a descendant of the ichthyosaur, and a monster himself. The upright lace of Venetian façades is the best line time-alias-water has left on terra firma anywhere. Plus, there is no doubt a correspondence between—if not an outright dependence on—the rectangular nature of that lace's displays—i.e., local buildings—and the anarchy of water that spurns the notion of shape. It is as though space, cognizant here more than anyplace else of its inferiority to time, answers it with the only property time doesn't possess: with beauty. And that's why water takes this answer, twists it, wallops and shreds it, but ultimately carries it by and large intact off into the Adriatic.

he eye in this city acquires an autonomy similar to that of a tear. The only difference is that it doesn't sever itself from the body but subordinates it totally. After a while—on the third or fourth day here—the body starts to regard itself as merely the eye's carrier, as a kind of submarine to its now di-

lating, now squinting periscope. Of course, for all its targets, its explosions are invariably self-inflicted: it's your own heart, or else your mind, that sinks; the eye pops up to the surface. This of course owes to the local topography, to the streets—narrow, meandering like eels—that finally bring you to a flounder of a *campo* with a cathedral in the middle of it, barnacled with saints and flaunting its Medusa-like cupolas. No matter what you set out for as you leave the house here, you are bound to get lost in these long, coiling lanes and passageways that beguile you to see them through, to follow them to their elusive end, which usually hits water, so that you can't even call it a cul-de-sac. On the map this city looks like two grilled fish sharing a plate, or perhaps like two nearly overlapping lobster claws (Pasternak compared it to a swollen croissant); but it has no north, south, east, or west; the only direction it has is sideways. It surrounds you like frozen seaweed, and the more you dart and dash about trying to get your bearings, the more you get lost. The yellow arrow signs at intersections are not much help either, for they, too, curve. In fact, they don't so much help you as kelp you. And in the fluently flapping hand of the native whom you stop to ask for directions, the eye, oblivious to his sputtering *A destra, a sinistra, dritto, dritto*, readily discerns a fish.

mesh caught in frozen seaweed might be a better metaphor. Because of the scarcity of space, people exist here in cellular proximity to one another, and life evolves with the immanent logic of gossip. One's territorial imperative in this city is circumscribed by water; the window shutters bar not so much daylight or noise (which is minimal here) as what may emanate from inside. When they are opened, shutters resemble the wings of angels prying into someone's sordid affairs, and like the spacing of the statues on cornices, human interplay here takes on the

aspects of jewelry or, better yet, filigree. In these parts one is both more secretive and better informed than the police in tyrannies. No sooner do you cross the threshold of your apartment, especially in winter, than you fall prey to every conceivable surmise, fantasy, rumor. If you've got company, the next day at the grocery or newsagent you may meet a stare of biblical probing unfathomable, you would think, in a Catholic country. If you sue someone here, or vice versa, you must hire a lawyer on the outside. A traveler, of course, enjoys this sort of thing; the native doesn't. What a painter sketches, or an amateur photographs, is no fun for the citizen. Yet insinuation as a principle of city planning (which notion locally emerges only with the benefit of hindsight) is better than any modern grid and in tune with the local canals, taking their cue from water, which, like the chatter behind you, never ends. In that sense, brick is undoubtedly more potent than marble, although both are unassailable for a stranger. However, once or twice over these seventeen years, I've managed to insinuate myself into a Venetian inner sanctum, into that beyond-the-amalgam labyrinth Régnier described in *Provincial Entertainments*. It happened in such a roundabout way that I can't even recall the details now, for I could not keep tabs on all those twists and turns that led to my passage into this labyrinth at the time. Somebody said something to somebody else, while the other person who wasn't even supposed to be there listened in and telephoned the fourth, as a result of which I'd been invited one night to a party given by the umpteenth at his palazzo.

he palazzo had become the umpteenth's only recently, after nearly three centuries of legal battles fought by several branches of a family that had given the world a couple of Venetian admirals. Accordingly,

two huge, splendidly carved aft-lanterns loomed in the two-story-high cave of the palazzo's courtyard, which was filled with all sorts of naval paraphernalia, dating from Renaissance days onward. The umpteenth himself, the last in the line, after decades and decades of waiting, had finally got it, to the great consternation of the other—apparently numerous—members of the family. He was no navy man; he was a bit of a playwright and a bit of a painter. For the moment, though, the most obvious thing about this forty-year-old —a slim, short creature in a gray double-breasted suit of very good cut—was that he was quite sick. His skin looked post-hepatitis, parchment yellow—or perhaps it was just an ulcer. He ate nothing but consommé and boiled vegetables while his guests were gorging themselves on what would qualify as a separate chapter, if not a book.

So the party was celebrating the umpteenth's having come into his own, as well as his launching a press to produce books about Venetian art. It was already in full swing when the three of us—a fellow writer, her son, and I—arrived. There were a lot of people: local and faintly international luminaries, politicos, nobles, the theater crowd, beards and ascots, mistresses of varying degrees of flamboyance, a bicycle star, American academics. Also, a bunch of giggling, agile, homosexual youths inevitable these days whenever something mildly spectacular takes place. They were presided over by a rather distraught and spiteful middle-aged queen—very blond, very blue-eyed, very drunk: the premises' major domo, whose days here were over and who therefore loathed everyone. Rightly so, I would add, given his prospects.

As they were making quite a ruckus, the umpteenth politely offered to show the three of us the rest of the house. We readily agreed and went up by a small elevator. When we left its cabin, we left the twentieth, the nineteenth, and a large portion of the eighteenth century behind, or, more accurately, below: like sediment at the bottom of a narrow shaft.

We found ourselves in a long, poorly lit gallery with a convex ceiling swarming with putti. No light would have helped anyway, as the walls were covered with large, floor-to-ceiling, dark-brownish oil paintings, definitely tailored to this space and separated by barely discernible marble busts and pilasters. The pictures depicted, as far as one could make out, sea and land battles, ceremonies, scenes from mythology; the lightest hue was wine-red. It was a mine of heavy porphyry in a state of abandonment, in a state of perpetual evening, with oils obscuring its ores; the silence here was truly geological. You couldn't ask, What is this? Who is this by? because of the incongruity of your voice, belonging to a later and obviously irrelevent organism. Or else it felt like an underwater journey—we were like a school of fish passing through a sunken galleon loaded with treasure, but not opening our mouths, since water would rush in.

At the far end of the gallery our host flitted to the right, and we followed him into a room which appeared to be a cross between the library and the study of a seventeenth-century gentleman. Judging by the books behind the criss-crossed wire in the red, wardrobe-size wooden cabinet, the gentleman's century could even have been the sixteenth. There were about sixty fat, white, vellum-bound volumes, from Aesop to Zeno; just enough for a gentleman; more would turn him into a penseur, with disastrous consequences either for his manners or for his estate. Other than that, the room was quite bare. The light in it wasn't much better than in the gallery; I'd made out a desk and a large faded globe. Then our host turned a knob and I saw his silhouette framed by a door leading into an enfilade. I glanced at that enfilade and I shuddered: it looked like a vicious, viscous infinity. I swallowed air and stepped into it.

It was a long succession of empty rooms. Rationally I knew that it couldn't be longer than the gallery parallel to which it ran. Yet it was. I had the sense of walking not so much in standard perspective as in a horizontal spiral where the laws of optics were suspended. Each room meant your further disappearance, the next degree of your nonexistence. This had to do with three things: drapery, mirrors, and dust. Although in some cases you could tell a room's designation—dining room, salon, possibly a nursery—most were similar in their lack of apparent function. They were about the same in size, or at any rate, they didn't seem to differ much in that way from one another. And in each one of them windows were draped and two or three mirrors adorned the walls.

Whatever the original color and pattern of the drapes had been, they now looked pale yellow and very brittle. A touch of your finger, let alone a breeze, would mean sheer destruction to them, as the shards of fabric scattered nearby on the parquet suggested. They were shedding, those curtains, and some of their folds exposed broad, bald, threadbare patches, as though the fabric felt it had come full circle and was now reverting to its pre-loom state. Our breath was perhaps too great an intimacy also; still, it was better than fresh oxygen, which, like history, the drapes didn't need. This was neither decay nor decomposition; this was dissipation back into time, where color and texture don't matter, where perhaps having learned what may happen to them, they will regroup and return, here or elsewhere, in a different guise. "Sorry," they seemed to say, "next time around we'll be more durable."

Then there were those mirrors, two or three in each room, of various sizes, but mostly rectangular. They all had delicate golden frames, with well-wrought floral garlands or idyllic scenes which called more attention to themselves than to their surface, since the amalgam was invariably in poor shape. In a sense, the frames were more coherent than their contents, straining, as it were, to keep them from spreading over the wall. Having grown unaccustomed over the centuries to reflecting anything but the wall opposite, the mirrors were quite reluctant to return one's visage, out of either greed or impotence, and when they tried, one's features would come back incomplete. I thought, I begin to understand Régnier. From room to room, as we proceeded through the enfilade, I saw myself in those frames less and less, getting back more and more darkness. Gradual subtraction, I thought to myself; how is this going to end? And it ended in the tenth or eleventh room. I stood by the door leading into the next chamber, staring at a largish, three-by-four-foot gilded rectangle, and instead of myself I saw pitch-black nothing. Deep and inviting, it seemed to contain a perspective of its own—perhaps another enfilade. For a moment I felt dizzy; but as I was no novelist, I skipped the option and took a doorway.

All along it had been reasonably ghostly;

now it became unreasonably so. The host and my companions lagged somewhere behind; I was on my own. There was a great deal of dust everywhere; the hues and shapes of everything in sight were mitigated by its gray. Marble inlaid tables, porcelain figurines, sofas, chairs, the very parquet. Everything was powdered with it, and sometimes, as with figurines and busts, the effect was oddly beneficial, accentuating their features, their folds, the vivacity of a group. But usually its layer was thick and solid; what's more, it had an air of finality, as though no new dust could be added to it. Every surface craves dust, for dust is the flesh of time, as a poet said, time's very flesh and blood; but here the craving seemed to be over. Now it will seep into the objects themselves, I thought, fuse with them, and in the end replace them. It depends of course on the material; some of it quite durable. They may not even disintegrate; they'll simply become grayer, as time would have nothing against assuming their shapes, the way it already had in this succession of vacuum chambers in which it was overtaking matter.

The last of them was the master bedroom. A gigantic yet uncovered four-poster bed dominated its space: the admiral's revenge for the narrow cot aboard his ship, or perhaps his homage to the sea itself. The latter was more probable, given the monstrous stucco cloud of putti descending on the bed and playing the role of baldachin. In fact, it was more sculpture than putti. The cherubs' faces were terribly grotesque: they all had these corrupt, lecherous grins as they stared—very keenly—downward upon the bed. They reminded me of that stable of giggling youths downstairs; and then I noticed a portable TV set in the corner of this otherwise absolutely bare room. I pictured the major domo entertaining his choice in this chamber: a writhing island of naked flesh amid a sea of linen, under the scrutiny of the dust-covered gypsum masterpiece. Oddly enough, I felt no repulsion. On the contrary, I felt that from time's point of view such entertainment here could only seem appropriate, as it generated nothing. After all, for three centuries, nothing here reigned supreme. Wars, revolutions, great discoveries, geniuses, plagues never entered here due to a legal problem. Causality was canceled, since its human carriers strolled in this perspective only in a caretaker capacity, once in a few years, if that. So the little wriggling shoal in the linen sea was, in fact, in tune with the premises, since it couldn't in nature give birth to anything. At best, the major domo's island—or should I say volcano?—existed only in the eyes of the putti. On the mirror's map it didn't. Neither did I.

hat happened only once, although I've been told there are scores of places like this in Venice. But once is enough, especially in winter, when the local fog, the famous *nebbia*, renders this place more extem-

poral than any palace's inner sanctum, by obliterating not only reflections but everything that has a shape: buildings, people, colonnades, bridges, statues. Boat services are canceled, airplanes neither arrive nor take off for weeks, stores are closed, and mail ceases to litter one's threshold. The effect is as though some raw hand had turned all those enfilades inside out and wrapped the lining around the city. Left, right, up, and down swap places, and you can find your way around only if you are a native or were given a cicerone. The fog is thick, blinding, and immobile. The latter aspect, however, is of advantage to you if you go out on a short errand, say, to get a pack of cigarettes, for you can find your way back via the tunnel your body has burrowed in the fog; the tunnel is likely to stay open for half an hour. This is a time for reading, for burning electricity all day long, for going easy on self-deprecating thoughts or coffee, for listening to the BBC World Service, for going to bed early.

In short, a time for self-oblivion, induced by a city that has ceased to be seen. Unwittingly, you take your cue from it, especially if, like it, you've got no company. Having failed to be born here, you at least can take some pride in sharing its invisibility.

n the whole, however, I've always been as keen on the contents of this city's average brick affairs as on those of the marbled and unique. There is nothing populist, let alone anti-aristocratic, to this preference; nor is there anything of the novelist. It's just the echo of the sort of houses I've lived or worked in for most of my life. Failing to have been born here, I've failed, I suppose, a bit further by picking up a line of work which normally doesn't land one on a *piano nobile*. On the other hand, there is perhaps some perverse snobbery in the sentiment for brick here, for its rank red akin to inflamed muscle bared by

the scabs of peeled-off stucco. Like eggs, which often—especially while I'm fixing myself breakfast—make me imagine the unknown civilization that came up with the idea of producing canned food in an organic fashion, brick and bricklaying somehow ring of an alternative order of flesh, not raw of course, but scarlet enough, and made up of small, identical cells. Yet another of the species' self-portraits at the elemental level, be it a wall or a chimney. In the end, like the Almighty Himself, we make everything in our image, for want of a more reliable model; our artifacts tell more about ourselves than our confessions.

t any rate, I seldom got myself across the thresholds of ordinary dwellings in this city. No tribe likes strangers, and Venetians are very tribal, in addition to being islanders. My Italian, wildly oscillating around its firm zero, also remained a deterrent. It always got better after a month or so, but then I'd be boarding the plane that would remove me from the opportunity to use it for another year. Therefore, the company I kept was that of English-speaking natives and expatriate Americans whose houses shared a familiar version—if not degree—of affluence. As for those who spoke Russian, the characters from the local U, their sentiments toward the country of my birth and their politics used to bring me to the brink of nausea. The result would be nearly the same with the two or three local authors and academics: too many abstract lithographs on the walls, too many tidy bookshelves and African trinkets, silent wives, sallow daughters, conversations running their moribund course through current events, someone else's fame, psychotherapy, surrealism, down to the description of a shortcut to my hotel. Disparity of pursuits compromised by tautology of net results, if one needs a formula, that is. I aspired to wasting my afternoons in the empty office of some local solicitor or pharmacist, eyeing his secretary as she brought in coffee from a bar nearby, chatting idly away about the prices of motorboats or the redeeming features of Diocletian's character, since practically everyone here has a reasonably sound education as well as a yen for things streamlined. I'd be unable to lift myself from the chair, his clients would be few; in the end, he'd lock up the premises and we'd stroll to the Gritti or Danieli, where I'd buy him drinks; if I was lucky, his secretary would join us. We'd sink in deep armchairs, exchanging malicious remarks about the new German battalions or the ubiquitous Japanese peeping through their cameras, like new elders, at the pallid naked marble thighs of this Susannah-like city wading cold, sunset-tinged, lapping waters. Later he might invite me over to his place for supper, and his pregnant wife, rising above the steaming pasta, would berate me volubly for my protracted bachelorhood . . . Too many neorealist movies, I suppose, too much Svevo-reading. For this sort of fantasy to come true, the requirements are the same as for inhabiting a *piano nobile*. I don't meet them, nor have I ever stayed here long enough to abandon this pipe dream entirely. To have another life, one ought to be able to wrap up the first one, and the job should be done neatly. No one pulls this sort of thing off convincingly, though, at times, good services are rendered to one either by absconding spouses or by political systems . . . It's the other houses, strange staircases, odd smells, unfamiliar furniture and topography that the proverbial old dogs dream about in their senility and decrepitude, not new masters. And the trick is not to disturb them.

o I never slept, let alone sinned, in a cast-iron family bed with pristine, crisp linen, embroidered and richly fringed bedspread, cloudlike pillows, and small pearl-encrusted crucifix above the headboard.

I never trained my vacant stare on an oleograph of the Madonna, or faded pictures of a father/brother/uncle/son in a *bersagliere* helmet, with its black feathers, or chintz curtains on the window, or porcelain or majolica jug atop a dark wood chest of drawers filled with local lace, sheets, towels, pillowcases, and underclothes washed and ironed on the kitchen table by a young, strong, tanned, almost swarthy arm, as a shoulder strap slips off it and silver beads of sweat sparkle on the forehead. (Speaking of silver, it would in all likelihood be tucked away under a pile of sheets in one of those drawers.) All this, of course, is from a movie in which I was neither a star nor even an extra, from a movie which for all I know they are not ever going to shoot again, or, if they do, the props will look different. In my mind, it is called *Nozze di Seppia*, and it's got no plot to it, save a scene with me walking along the Fondamente Nuove with the greatest watercolor in the world on the left and a red-brick infinity on the right. I should be wearing a cloth cap, dark serge jacket, and a white shirt with an open collar, washed and ironed by the same strong, tanned hand. Approaching the Arsenale, I'd turn right, cross twelve bridges, and take via Garibaldi to the Giardini, where, on an iron chair in the Caffè Paradiso, would be sitting she who washed and ironed this shirt six years ago. She'd have before her a glass of *chinotto* and a *panino*, a frayed little volume of Propertius' *Monobiblos* or Pushkin's *Captain's Daughter*; she'd be wearing a knee-length taffeta dress bought once in Rome on the eve of our trip to Ischia. She would lift her eyes, the color of mustard and honey, fix them on the figure in the heavy serge jacket, and say, "What a belly!" If anything is to save this picture from being a flop, it will be the winter light.

while ago I saw somewhere a photograph of a wartime execution. Three pale, skinny men of medium height and no specific facial features (they were seen by the camera in profile) stood on the edge of a freshly dug ditch. They had a Northern appearance—in fact, I think the photograph was taken in Lithuania. Close behind each one of them stood a German soldier holding a pistol. In the distance you could make out a bunch of other soldiers: the onlookers. It looked like early winter or late autumn, as the soldiers were in their winter overcoats. The condemned men, all three of them, were also dressed identically. They wore cloth caps, heavy black jackets over white undershirts without collars: victims' uniform. On top of everything, they were cold. Partly because of that they drew their heads into their shoulders. In a second they will die: the photographer pushed his button an instant before the soldiers pulled their triggers. The

three village lads drew their heads into their shoulders and were squinting the way a child does anticipating pain. They expected to be hurt, perhaps badly hurt; they expected the deafening—so close to their ears!—sound of a shot. And they squinted. Because the human repertoire of responses is so limited! What was coming to them was death, not pain; yet their bodies couldn't distinguish one from the other.

ne afternoon in November 1977, in the Londra, where I was staying courtesy of the Biennale on Dissent, I received a phone call from Susan Sontag, who was staying in the Gritti under the same dispensation. "Joseph," she said, "what are you doing this evening?" "Nothing," I said. "Why?" "Well, I bumped into Olga Rudge today in the piazza. Do you know her?" "No. You mean the Pound woman?" "Yes," said

Susan, "and she invited me over tonight. I dread going there alone. Would you go with me, if you haven't got other plans?" I had none, and I said, Sure, I will, having understood her apprehension only too well. Mine, I thought, could be even greater. Well, to begin with, in my line of work Ezra Pound is a big deal, practically an industry. Many an American graphomaniac has found in Ezra Pound both a master and a martyr. As a young man, I had translated quite a bit of him into Russian. The translations were trash, but came very close to being published, courtesy of some crypto-Nazi on the board of a solid literary magazine (now, of course, the man is an avid nationalist). I liked the original for its sophomoric freshness and taut verse, for its thematic and stylistic diversity, for its voluminous cultural references, then out of my reach. I also liked his "make it new" dictum—liked it, that is, until I grasped that the true reason for making it new was that "it" was fairly old; that we were, after all, in a body shop. As for his plight in St. Elizabeths, in Russian eyes, that was nothing to rave about and, anyhow, better than the nine grams of lead that his wartime radio spiels might have earned him elsewhere. *The Cantos*, too, left me cold; the main error was an old one: questing after beauty. For someone with such a long record of residence in Italy, it was odd that he hadn't realized that beauty can't be targeted, that it is always a by-product of other, often very ordinary pursuits. A fair thing to do, I thought, would be to publish both his poems and his speeches in one volume, without any learned introduction, and see what happens. Of all people, a poet should have known that time knows no distance between Rapallo and Lithuania. I also thought that admitting that you've screwed up your life is more manly than persevering in the posture of a persecuted genius, with all the throwing up of the arm in a Fascist salute upon his return to Italy, subsequent disclaimers of the gesture's significance, reticent interviews, and cape and staff cultivating the appearance of a sage with the net result of resembling Haile Selassie. He was still big with some of my friends, and now I was to see his old woman.

The address given was in the Salute sestiere, the part of town with the greatest, to my knowledge, percentage of foreigners in it, Anglos especially. After some meandering, we found the place—not too far, in fact, from the house in which Régnier dwelt in the teens of the century. We rang the bell, and the first thing I saw after the little woman with the beady eyes took shape on the threshold was the poet's bust by Gaudier-Brzeska sitting on the floor of the drawing room. The grip of boredom was sudden but sure.

Tea was served, but no sooner had we taken the first sip than the hostess—a gray-haired, diminutive, shipshape lady with many years in her to go—lifted her sharp finger, which slid into an invisible mental groove, and out of her pursed lips came an aria the score of which has been in the public domain at least since 1945. That Ezra wasn't a Fascist; that they were afraid the Americans (which sounded pretty strange coming from an American) would put him in the chair; that he knew nothing about what was going on; that there were no Germans in Rapallo; that he'd travel from Rapallo to Rome only twice a month for the broadcast; that the Americans, again, were wrong to think that Ezra meant it to . . . At some point I stopped registering what she was saying—which is easy for me, as English is not my mother tongue —and just nodded in the pauses, or whenever she'd punctuate her monologue with a tic-like *"Capito?"* A record, I thought; her master's voice. Be polite and don't interrupt the lady; it's garbage, but she believes it. There is something in me, I suppose, that always respects the physical side of human utterance, regardless of the content; the very movement of someone's lips is more essential than what moves them. I sank deeper into my armchair and tried to concentrate on the cookies, as there was no dinner.

What woke me from my reverie was the sound of Susan's voice, which meant that the record had come to a stop. There was something odd in her timbre and I cocked my ear. Susan was saying, "But surely, Olga, you don't think that the Americans got cross with Ezra over his broadcasts. Because if it were only his broadcasts, then Ezra would be just another Tokyo Rose." Now, that was one of the greatest returns I had ever heard. I looked at Olga. It must be said that she took it like a mensch. Or, better yet, a pro. Or else she didn't grasp what Susan had said, though I doubt it. "What was it, then?" she inquired. "It was Ezra's anti-Semitism," replied Susan, and I saw the corundum needle of the old lady's finger once again hitting the groove. On this side of the record was: "One should realize that Ezra was not an anti-Semite; that after all his name was *Ezra*; that some of his friends were Jewish, including one Venetian admiral; that . . ." The tune was equally familiar and equally long—about three-quarters of an hour; but this time we had to go. We thanked the old lady for the evening and bade her farewell. I, for one, did not feel the sadness one usually feels leaving the house of a widow—or for that matter anybody alone in an empty place. The old lady was in good shape, reasonably well off; on top of that, she had the comfort of her convictions—a comfort, I felt, she'd go to any length to defend. I think I'd never met a Fascist—young or old; however, I'd dealt with a considerable number of old CP members, and that's why tea at Olga Rudge's place, with that bust of Ezra sitting on the floor, rang, so to speak, a bell. We turned to the left of the house and two minutes later found ourselves on the Fondamenta degli Incurabili.

h, the good old suggestive power of language! Ah, this legendary ability of words to imply more than reality can provide! Ah, the lock, stock, and barrel of the métier. Of course, the "Embankment of the Incurables" harks back to the plague, to the epidemics that used to sweep this city half clean century after century with a census taker's regularity. The name conjures the hopeless cases, not so much strolling along as scattered about on the flagstones, literally expiring, shrouded, waiting to be carted—or, rather, shipped away. Torches, fumes, gauze masks preventing inhalation, rustling of monks' frocks and habits, soaring black capes, candles. Gradually the funereal procession turns into a carnival, or indeed a promenade, where a mask would have to be worn, since in this city everybody knows everybody. Add to this, tubercular poets and composers; add to this, men of moronic convictions or aesthetes hopelessly en-

amored of this place—and the embankment might earn its name, reality might catch up with language. And add to this that the interplay between plague and literature (poetry in particular, and Italian poetry especially) was quite intricate from the threshold. That Dante's descent into the netherworld owes as much to Homer's and Virgil's—episodic scenes, after all, in the *Iliad* and the *Aeneid*—as to Byzantine medieval literature about cholera, with its traditional conceit of premature burial and subsequent peregrination of the soul. Overzealous agents of the netherworld bustling around the cholera-stricken city would often zero in on a badly dehydrated body, put their lips to his nostrils, and suck away his life spirit, thereby proclaiming him dead and fit to be buried. Once underneath, the individual would pass through infinite halls and chambers, pleading that he has been consigned to the realm of the dead unjustly and seeking redress. Upon obtaining it—usually by facing a tribunal presided over by Hippocrates—he would return full of stories about those he had bumped into in the halls and chambers below: kings, queens, heroes, famous or infamous mortals of his time, repentant, resigned, defiant. Sounds familiar? Well, so much for the suggestive powers of the métier. One never knows what engenders what: an experience a language, or a language an experience. Both are capable of generating quite a lot. When one is badly sick, one imagines all sorts of consequences and developments which, for all we know, won't ever take place. Is this metaphoric thinking? The answer, I believe, is yes. Except that when one is sick, one hopes, even against hope, to get cured, the illness to stop. The end of an illness thus is the end of its metaphors. A metaphor—or, to put it more broadly, language itself—is by and large open-ended, it craves continuum: an afterlife, if you will. In other words (no pun intended), metaphor is incurable. Add then to all of this yourself, a carrier of this métier, or of this virus—in fact, of a couple of them, sharpening your teeth for a third—shuffling on a windy night along the Fondamenta, whose name proclaims your diagnosis regardless of the nature of your malady.

he winter light in this city! It has the extraordinary property of enhancing your eye's power of resolution to the point of microscopic precision—the pupil, especially when it is of the gray or mustard-and-honey variety, humbles any Hasselblad lens and develops your subsequent memories to a *National Geographic* sharpness. The sky is brisk blue; the sun, escaping its golden likeness beneath the foot of San Giorgio, sashays over the countless fish scales of the *laguna*'s lapping ripples; behind you, under the colonnades of the Palazzo Ducale, a bunch of stocky fellows in fur coats are revving up *Eine Kleine Nachtmusik*, just for you, slumped in your white chair and squinting at the pigeons' maddening gambits on the

chessboard of a vast *campo*. The espresso at your cup's bottom is the one black dot in, you feel, a miles-long radius. Such are the noons here. In the morning this light breasts your windowpane and, having pried your eye open like a shell, runs ahead of you, strumming its lengthy rays—like a hot-footed schoolboy running his stick along the iron grate of a park or garden—along arcades, colonnades, red-brick chimneys, saints, and lions. "Depict! Depict!" it cries to you, either mistaking you for some Canaletto or Carpaccio or Guardi, or because it doesn't trust your retina's ability to retain what it makes available, not to mention your brain's capacity to absorb it. Perhaps the latter explains the former. Perhaps they are synonymous. Perhaps art is simply an organism's reaction against its retentive limitations. At any rate, you obey the command and grab your camera, supplementing both your brain cells and your pupil. Should this city ever be short of cash, it can go straight to Kodak for assistance—or else tax its products savagely.

By the same token, as long as this place exists, as long as winter light shines upon it, Kodak shares are the best investment.

t sunset all cities look wonderful, but some more so than others. Reliefs become suppler, columns more rotund, capitals curlier, cornices more resolute, spires starker, niches deeper, disciples more draped, angels airborne. In the streets it gets dark, but it is still daytime for the Fondamenta and that gigantic liquid mirror where motorboats, vaporetti, gondolas, dinghies, and barges "like scattered old shoes" zealously trample Baroque and Gothic façades, not sparing your own or a passing cloud's reflection either. "Depict it," whispers the winter light, stopped flat by the brick wall of a hospital or arriving home at the paradise of San Zaccaria's *frontone* after its long passage through the cosmos. And you sense

this light's fatigue as it rests in Zaccaria's marble shells for another hour or so, while the earth is turning its other cheek to the luminary. This is the winter light at its purest. It carries no warmth or energy, having shed them and left them behind somewhere in the universe, or in the nearby cumulus. Its particles' only ambition is to reach an object and make it, big or small, visible. It's a private light, the light of Giorgione or Bellini, not the light of Tiepolo or Tintoretto. And the city lingers in it, savoring its touch, the caress of the infinity whence it came. An object, after all, is what makes infinity private.

nd the object can be a little monster, with the head of a lion and the body of a dolphin. The latter would coil, the former gnash its fangs. It could adorn an entrance or simply burst out of a wall without any ap-

parent purpose, the absence of which would make it oddly recognizable. In a certain line of work, and at a certain age, nothing is more recognizable than a lack of purpose. The same goes for a fusion of two or more traits or properties, not to mention genders. On the whole, all these nightmarish creatures—dragons, gargoyles, basilisks, female-breasted sphinxes, winged lions, Cerberuses, Minotaurs, centaurs, chimeras—that come to us from mythology (which, by rights, should have the status of classical surrealism) are our self-portraits, in the sense that they denote the species' genetic memory of evolution. Small wonder that here, in this city sprung from water, they abound. Again, there is nothing Freudian to them, nothing sub- or unconscious. Given the nature of human reality, the interpretation of dreams is a tautology and at best could be justified only by daylight's ratio to darkness. It's doubtful, though, that this democratic principle is operational in nature, where nothing enjoys a majority. Not even water, though it reflects and refracts everything, including itself, alternating forms and substances, sometimes gently, sometimes monstrously. That's what accounts for the quality of winter light here; that's what explains its fondness for little monsters, as well as for cherubs. Presumably cherubs, too, are part of the species' evolution. Or else it is the other way around, for if one was to take their census in this city, they might outnumber the natives.

onsters, however, command more of one's attention. If only because this term has been hurled at one more frequently than the other; if only because in our parts one gains wings only in the air force. One's guilty conscience would be enough to identify oneself with any of these marble, bronze, or plaster concoctions—with

the dragon, to say the least, rather than with San Giorgio. In a line of work involving the dipping of a pen into an inkpot, one can identify with both. After all, there is no saint without a monster—not to mention the ink's octopal affinity. But even without reflecting upon or refracting this idea, it is clear that this is a city of fish, caught and swimming around alike. And seen by a fish—endowed, let's say, with a human eye, in order to avoid its own famous distortion—man would appear a monster indeed; not an octopus, perhaps, but surely a quadropus. Something, to say the least, far more complex than the fish itself. Small wonder, then, that sharks are after us so much. Should one ask a simple *orata*—not even a caught one, in a free state—what it thinks one looks like, it will reply, You are a monster. And the conviction in its voice will be oddly familiar, as though its eye is of the mustard-and-honey variety.

o you never know as you move through these labyrinths whether you are pursuing a goal or running from yourself, whether you are the hunter or his prey. Surely not a saint, but perhaps not yet a full-scale dragon; hardly a Theseus, but not a maiden-starved Minotaur either. The Greek version rings, though, a better bell, since the winner gets nothing, because the slayer and the slain are related. The monster, after all, was the prize's half brother; in any case, he was half brother to the hero's eventual wife. Ariadne and Phaedra were sisters, and for all we know, the brave Athenian had them both. In fact, with an eye on marrying into the Cretan king's family, he might have accepted the murderous commission to make the family more respectable. As granddaughters of Helios, the girls were supposed to be pure and shining; their names suggested as much. Why, even their mother, Pasiphaë, was, for all her dark urges,

Blindingly Bright. And perhaps she yielded to those dark urges and did it with the bull precisely to prove that nature neglects the majority principle, since the bull's horns suggest the moon. Perhaps she was interested in chiaroscuro rather than in bestiality and eclipsed the bull for purely optical reasons. And the fact that the bull, whose symbolism-laden pedigree ran all the way back to cave paintings, was blind enough to mistake the artificial cow Daedalus built for Pasiphaë on this occasion is her proof that her ancestry still holds the upper hand in the system of causality, that Helios' light, refracted in her, Pasiphaë, is still—after four children (two fine daughters and two good-for-nothing boys)—blindingly bright. As far as the principle of causality is concerned, it should be added that the main hero in this story is precisely Daedalus, who, apart from a very convincing cow, built—this time on the king's request—the very labyrinth in which the bull-headed offspring and his slayer got to face each other one day, with disastrous consequences for the former. In a manner of speaking, the whole business is Daedalus' brain child, the labyrinth especially, as it resembles a brain. In a manner of speaking, everybody is related to everybody, the pursuer to the pursued, at least. Small wonder, then, that one's meanderings through the streets of this city, whose biggest colony for nearly three centuries was the island of Crete, feels somewhat tautological, especially as light fades—that is, especially as its pasiphaian, ariadnan, and phaedran properties fail. In other words, especially in the evening, when one loses oneself to self-deprecation.

n the brighter side there are, of course, lots of lions: winged ones, with their books opened on "Peace upon you, St. Mark the Evangelist," or lions of regular feline appearance. The winged ones, strictly speaking, belong in the category of monsters, too. Given

my occupation, however, I've always regarded them as a more agile and literate form of Pegasus, who can surely fly, but whose ability to read is somewhat more doubtful. A paw, at any rate, is a better instrument for turning pages than a hoof. In this city the lions are ubiquitous, and over the years I've unwittingly come to share this totem to the point of placing one of them on the cover of one of my books: the closest a man gets in my line of work to having his own façade. Yet monsters they are, if only because they are products of the city's fantasy, since even at the zenith of this republic's maritime might it controlled no territory where this animal could be found even in its wingless state. (The Greeks were more on the dot with their bull, its neolithic pedigree notwithstanding.) As for the Evangelist himself, he of course died in Alexandria, Egypt—but of natural causes—and he never went on a safari. In general, Christendom's truck with lions is negligible, as they could not be found in its domain, dwelling solely in Africa, and in deserts at that. This of course helped toward their subsequent association with desert fathers; other than that, the Christians could have encountered the animal only as its diet in Roman circuses, where lions were imported from African shores for entertainment. Their unfamiliarity—better to say, their nonexistence— was what would unleash the ancients' fantasy, enabling them to attribute to the animals various aspects of otherworldliness, including those of divine commerce. So it's not entirely wild to have this animal sitting on Venetian façades in the unlikely role of the guardian of St. Mark's eternal repose; if not the Church, then the city itself could be seen as a lioness protecting its cub. Besides, in this city, the Church and the state have merged, in a perfectly Byzantine fashion. The only case, I must add, where such a merger turned out—quite early on—to be to the subjects' advantage. No wonder, then, that the place was literally lionized, that the lion itself got lionized, which is to say humanized. On every cornice, over nearly every entrance, you see either its muzzle, with a human look, or a human head with leonine features. Both, in the final analysis, qualify as monsters (albeit of the benevolent sort), since neither ever existed. Also, because of their numerical superiority over any other carved or sculpted image, including that of the Madonna or the Redeemer Himself. On the other hand, it's easier to carve a beast than a human figure. Basically, the animal kingdom fared poorly in Christian art—not to mention the doctrine. So the local pride of *Felidae* may regard itself as their kingdom's way of getting even. In winter, they brighten one's dusk.

nce, in a dusk that darkened gray pupils but brought gold to those of the mustard-cum-honey variety, the owner of the latter and I encountered an Egyptian warship—a light cruiser, to be precise—

moored at the Fondamenta dell'Arsenale, near the Giardini. I can't recall its name now, but its home port was definitely Alexandria. It was a highly modern piece of naval hardware, bristling with all sorts of antennae, radar, satellite dishes, rocket launchers, antiaircraft turrets, etc., apart from the usual large-caliber guns. From a distance you couldn't tell its nationality. Even close up you could be confused, because the uniforms and general deportment of the crew aboard looked vaguely British. The flag was already lowered, and the sky over the *laguna* was changing from Bordeaux to dark porphyry. As we marveled at the nature of the errand that brought this man-of-war here—a need for repairs? a new courtship between Venice and Alexandria? to reclaim the holy relic stolen from the latter in the twelfth century? —its loudspeakers suddenly came to life and we heard, "Allah! Akbar Allah! Akbar!" The muezzin was calling the crew to evening prayer, the ship's two masts momentarily turning to minarets. All at once the cruiser was Istanbul in profile. I felt that the map had suddenly folded or the book of history had shut before my eyes. At least that it had become six centuries shorter: Christianity was no longer Islam's senior. The Bosporus was overlapping the Adriatic, and you couldn't tell which wave was which. A far cry from architecture.

n winter evenings the sea, welled by a contrary easterly, fills every canal to the brim like a bathtub, and at times overflows them. Nobody runs up from downstairs crying, "The pipes!" as there is no downstairs. The city stands ankle-deep in water, and boats, "hitched like animals to the walls," to quote Cassiodorus, prance. The pilgrim's shoe, having tested the water, is drying atop his hotel room's radiator; the native dives into

his closet to fish out his pair of rubber boots. "*Acqua alta*," says a voice over the radio, and human traffic subsides. Streets empty; stores, bars, restaurants and trattorias close. Only their signs continue burning, finally getting a piece of the narcissistic action as the pavement briefly, superficially, catches up with the canals. Churches, however, remain open, but then treading upon water is no news to either clergy or parishioners; neither to music, water's twin.

Seventeen years ago, wading aimlessly through one *campo* after another, a pair of green rubber boots brought me to the threshold of a smallish pink edifice. On its wall I saw a plaque saying that Antonio Vivaldi, prematurely born, was baptized in this church. In those days I was still reasonably red-haired; I felt sentimental about bumping into the place of baptism of that "red cleric" who has given me so much joy on so many occasions and in so many godforsaken parts of the world. And I seemed to recall that it was Olga Rudge who had organized the first-ever Vivaldi *settimana* in this city—as it happened, just a few days before World War II broke out. It took place, somebody told me, in the palazzo of the Countess Polignac, and Miss Rudge was playing the violin. As she proceeded with the piece, she noticed out of the corner of her eye that a gentleman had entered the *salone* and stood by the door, since all the seats were taken. The piece was long, and now she felt somewhat worried, because she was approaching a passage where she had to turn the page without interrupting her play. The man in the corner of her eye started to move and soon disappeared from her field of vision. The passage grew closer, and her nervousness grew, too. Then, at exactly the point where she had to turn the page, a hand emerged from the left, stretched to the music stand, and slowly turned the sheet. She kept playing and, when the difficult passage was over, lifted her eyes to the left to acknowledge her gratitude. "And that," Olga Rudge told a friend of mine, "is how I first met Stravinsky."

o you may enter and stand through the service. The singing will be a bit subdued, presumably on account of the weather. If you can excuse it in this way, so, no doubt, will its Addressee. Besides, you can't follow it that well, whether it's in Italian or Latin. So you just stand or take a pew in the rear and listen. "The best way to hear Mass," Wystan Auden used to say, "is when you don't know the language." True, ignorance helps concentration on such occasions no less than the poor lighting from which the pilgrim suffers in every Italian church, especially in winter. Dropping coins into an illumination box while the service is in progress is not nice. What's more, you often don't have enough of

them in your pocket to appreciate the picture fully. In days of yore I carried with me a powerful, New-York-City-Police-Department-issue flashlight. One way to get rich, I thought, would be to start manufacturing miniature flashbulbs like those they mount on cameras, but of great duration. I'd call it "Lasting Flash," or, better yet, "*Fiat Lux*," and in a couple of years I'd buy an apartment somewhere in San Lio or Salute. I'd even marry my partner's secretary, which he doesn't have since he doesn't exist . . . The music subsides; its twin, however, has risen, you discover upon stepping outside—not significantly, but enough for you to feel reimbursed for the faded chorale. For water, too, is choral, in more ways than one. It is the same water that carried the Crusaders, the merchants, St. Mark's relics, Turks, every kind of cargo, military, or pleasure vessel; above all, it reflected everybody who ever lived, not to mention stayed, in this city, everybody who ever strolled or waded its streets in the way you do now. Small wonder that it looks muddy green in the daytime and pitch black at night, rivaling the firmament. A miracle that, rubbed the right and the wrong way for over a millennium, it doesn't have holes in it, that it is still H_2O, though you would never drink it; that it still rises. It really does look like musical sheets, frayed at the edges, constantly played, coming to you in tidal scores, in bars of canals with innumerable obbligati of bridges, mullioned windows, or curved crownings of Coducci cathedrals, not to mention the violin necks of gondolas. In fact, the whole city, especially at night, resembles a gigantic orchestra, with dimly lit music stands of palazzi, with a restless chorus of waves, with the falsetto of a star in the winter sky. The music is, of course, greater than the band, and no hand can turn the page.

hat's what worries the band, or more exactly, its conductors, the city fathers. According to their calculations, this city, during this century alone, has sagged twenty-three centimeters. So what appears spectacular to the tourist is a full-scale headache for the native. And if it were only a headache, that would be fine. But the headache is crowned with an increasing apprehension, not to say fear, that what lies in store for the city is the fate of Atlantis. The fear is not without foundation, and not only because the city's uniqueness does amount to a civilization of its own. The main danger is perceived to be high winter tides; the rest is done by the mainland's industry and agriculture silting the *laguna* with their chemical wastes, and by the deterioration of the city's own clogged canals. In my line of work, though, ever since the Romantics, human fault has appeared to be a likelier culprit when it comes to disaster than any *forza del*

destino. (That an insurance man can tell these two apart is indeed a feat of imagination.) So, prey to tyrannical impulses, I would install some sort of flap gate to stem the sea of humanity, which has swelled in the last two decades by two billion and whose crest is its refuse. I'd freeze the industry and the residence in the twenty-mile zone along the northern shore of the *laguna*, drag and dredge the city's canals (I'd either use the military to carry out this operation or pay local companies double time) and seed them with fish and the right kind of bacteria to keep them clean.

I have no idea what kind of fish or bacteria these are, but I'm pretty sure they exist: tyranny is seldom synonymous with expertise. At any rate, I'd call Sweden and ask the Stockholm municipality for advice: in that city, with all its industry and population, the moment you step out of your hotel, the salmon leap out of the water to greet you. If it is the difference in temperature that does it, then one could try dumping blocks of ice into the canals or, failing that, routinely void the natives' freezers of ice cubes, since whiskey is not very much in vogue here, not even in winter.

"Why, then, do you go there at such a season?" my editor asked me once, sitting in a Chinese restaurant in New York with his gay English charges. "Yes, why do you?" they echoed their prospective benefactor. "What is it like there in winter?" I thought of telling them about *acqua alta*; about the various shades of gray in the window as one sits at breakfast in one's hotel, enveloped by silence and the mealy morning pall of newlyweds' faces; about pigeons accentuating every curve and cornice of the local Baroque in their dormant affinity for architecture; about a lonely monument to Francesco Querini and his two huskies carved out of Istrian stone similar, I think, in its hue, to what he saw last, dying, on his ill-fated journey to the North Pole, now listening to the Giardini's rustle of evergreens in the company of Wagner and Carducci; about a brave sparrow perching on the bobbing blade of a gondola against the backdrop of a sirocco-roiled damp infinity. No, I thought, looking at their effete but eager faces; no, that won't do. "Well," I said, "it's like Greta Garbo swimming."

ver these years, during my long stays and brief sojourns here, I have been, I think, both happy and unhappy in nearly equal measure. It didn't matter which, if only because I came here not for romantic purposes but to work, to finish a piece, to translate, to write a couple of poems, provided I could be that lucky; simply to be. That is, neither for a honeymoon (the closest I ever came to that was many years ago, on the island of Ischia, or else in Siena) nor for a divorce. And so I worked. Happiness or unhappiness would simply come

in attendance, although sometimes they'd stay longer than I did, as if waiting on me. It is a virtue, I came to believe long ago, not to make a meal out of one's emotional life. There's always enough work to do, not to mention that there's world enough outside. In the end, there's always this city. As long as it exists, I don't believe that I, or, for that matter, anyone, can be mesmerized or blinded by romantic tragedy. I remember one day—the day I had to leave after a month here alone. I had just had lunch in some small trattoria on the remotest part of the Fondamente Nuove, grilled fish and half a bottle of wine. With that inside, I set out for the place I was staying, to collect my bags and catch a vaporetto. I walked a quarter of a mile along the Fondamente Nuove, a small moving dot in that gigantic watercolor, and then turned right by the hospital of Giovanni e Paolo. The day was warm, sunny, the sky blue, all lovely. And with my back to the Fondamente and San Michele, hugging the wall of the hospital, almost rubbing it with my left shoulder and squinting at the sun, I suddenly felt: I am a cat. A cat that has just had fish. Had anyone addressed me at that moment, I would have meowed. I was absolutely, animally happy. Twelve hours later, of course, having landed in New York, I hit the worst possible mess in my life—or the one that appeared that way at the time. Yet the cat in me lingered; had it not been for that cat, I'd be climbing the walls now in some expensive institution.

t night, there is not much to do here. Opera and church recitals are options, of course, but they require some initiative and arrangement: tickets and schedules and so forth. I am not good at that; it's rather like fixing a three-course meal all for yourself—perhaps even lonelier. Besides, my luck is such

that whenever I considered an evening at La Fenice, they would be having a week-long run of Tchaikovsky or Wagner—equals, as far as my allergy is concerned. Never once Donizetti or Mozart! That leaves reading and strolling dully along, which is about the same, since at night these narrow stony gennels are like passages between the bookshelves of some immense, forgotten library, and equally quiet. All the "books" are shut tight, and you guess what they are about only by the names on their spines, under the doorbell. Oh, there you can find your Donizettis and Rossinis, your Lullys and Frescobaldis! Maybe even a Mozart, maybe even a Haydn. Or else these streets are like wardrobe racks: all the clothes are of dark, peeling fabric, but the lining is ruby and shimmering gold. Goethe called this place the "republic of beavers," but perhaps Montesquieu with his resolute "*un endroit ou il devrait n'avoir que des poissons*" was more on the mark. For, now and then, across the canal, two or three well-lit, tall, rounded windows, half shaded with gauze or tulle, reveal an octopal chandelier, the lacquered fin of a grand piano, opulent bronze framing auburn or rubescent oils, the gilded rib cage of a ceiling's beams—and you feel as though you are looking into a fish through its scales, and inside of it there's a party.

At a distance—across a canal—you can hardly tell the guests from their hostess. With all due respect to the best available creed, I must say I don't think this place has evolved from the famous chordate only, triumphant or not. I suspect and submit that, in the first place, it evolved from the very element that gave that chordate life and shelter and which, for me at least, is synonymous with time. The element comes in many shapes and hues, with many different properties apart from those of Aphrodite and the Redeemer: lull, storm, crest, wave, froth, ripple, etc., not to mention the marine organisms. In my mind, this city limns all discernible patterns of the element and its contents. Splashing, glittering, glowing, glinting, the element has been casting itself upward for so long that it is not surprising that some of these aspects eventually acquired mass, flesh, and grew solid. Why it should have happened here, I have no idea. Presumably because the element here had heard Italian.

he eye is the most autonomous of our organs. It is so because the objects of its attention are inevitably situated on the outside. Except in a mirror, the eye never sees itself. It is the last to shut down when the body is falling asleep. It stays open when the body is stricken with paralysis or dead. The eye keeps registering reality even when there is no apparent reason for doing this, and under all circumstances. The question is: Why? And the answer is: Because the environment is hostile.

Eyesight is the instrument of adjustment to an environment which remains hostile no matter how well you have adjusted to it. The hostility of the environment grows proportionately to the length of your presence in it, and I am speaking not of old age only. In short, the eye is looking for safety. That explains the eye's predilection for art in general and Venetian art in particular. That explains the eye's appetite for beauty, as well as beauty's own existence. For beauty is solace, since beauty is safe. It doesn't threaten you with murder or make you sick. A statue of Apollo doesn't bite, nor will Carpaccio's poodle. When the eye fails to find beauty—alias solace—it commands the body to create it, or, failing that, adjusts itself to perceive virtue in ugliness. In the first instance, it relies on human genius; in the second, it draws on one's reservoir of humility. The latter is in greater supply, and like every majority tends to make laws. Let's have an illustration; let's take a young maiden. At a certain age one eyes passing maidens without applied interest, without aspiring to mount them. Like a TV set left switched on in an abandoned apartment, the eye keeps sending in images of all these 5'8" miracles, complete with light chestnut hair, Perugino ovals, gazelle eyes, nurselike bosoms, wasp waists, dark-green velvet dresses, and razor-sharp tendons. An eye may zero in on them in a church at someone's wedding or, worse still, in a bookstore's poetry section. Reasonably farsighted or resorting to the counsel of the ear, the eye may learn their identities (which come with names as breathtaking as, say, Arabella Ferri) and, alas, their dishearteningly firm romantic affiliations. Regardless of such data's uselessness, the eye keeps collecting it. In fact, the more useless the data, the sharper the focus. The question is why, and the answer is that beauty is always external; also, that it is the exception to the rule. That's what—its location and its singularity—sends the eye oscillating wildly or—in militant humility's parlance—roving. For beauty is where the eye rests. Aesthetic sense is the twin of one's instinct for self-preservation and is more reliable than ethics. Aesthetics' main tool, the eye, is absolutely autonomous. In its autonomy, it is inferior only to a tear.

tear can be shed in this place on several occasions. Assuming that beauty is the distribution of light in the fashion most congenial to one's retina, a tear is an acknowledgment of the retina's, as well as the tear's, failure to retain beauty. On the whole, love comes with the speed of light; separation, with that of sound. It is the deterioration of the greater speed to the lesser that moistens one's eye. Because one is finite, a departure from this place always feels final; leaving it behind is leaving it forever. For leaving is a

banishment of the eye to the provinces of the other senses; at best, to the crevices and crevasses of the brain. For the eye identifies itself not with the body it belongs to but with the object of its attention. And to the eye, for purely optical reasons, departure is not the body leaving the city but the city abandoning the pupil. Likewise, disappearance of the beloved, especially a gradual one, causes grief no matter who, and for what peripatetic reason, is actually in motion. As the world goes, this city is the eye's beloved. After it, everything is a letdown. A tear is the anticipation of the eye's future.

o be sure, everybody has designs on her, on this city. Politicians and big businesses especially, for nothing has a greater future than money. It is so much so that money feels synonymous with the future

and tries to order it. Hence the wealth of frothy outpourings about revamping the city, about turning the entire province of Veneto into a gateway to Central Europe, about boosting the region's industry, expanding the harbor complex at Marghera, increasing the oil-tanker traffic in the *laguna* and deepening the *laguna* for the same purposes, about converting the Venetian Arsenale, immortalized by Dante, into the Beaubourg's spitting—literally—image for storing the most recently discharged phlegm, about housing an Expo here in the year 2000, etc. All this drivel normally gushes out of the same mouth, and often on the same breath, that blabbers about ecology, protection, restoration, cultural patrimony, and whatnot. The goal of all that is one: rape. No rapist, though, wants to regard himself as such, let alone get caught. Hence the mixture of objectives and metaphors, high rhetoric and lyrical fervor swelling the barrel chests of parliamentary deputies and *commendatore* alike.

Yet while these characters are far more dangerous—indeed more harmful—than the Turks, the Austrians, and Napoleon all lumped together, since money has more battalions than generals, in the seventeen years that I've frequented this city very little has changed here. What saves Venice, like Penelope, from her suitors is their rivalry, the competitive nature of capitalism boiled down to fat cats' blood relations to different political parties. Lobbing spanners into each other's machinery is something democracy is awfully good at, and the leapfrogging of Italian cabinets has proved to be the city's best insurance. So has the mosaic of the city's own political jigsaw. There are no doges anymore, and the 80,000 dwellers of these 118 islands are guided not by the grandeur of some particular vision but by their immediate, often nearsighted concerns, by their desire to make ends meet.

Farsightedness here, however, would be counterproductive. In a place this size, twenty or thirty people out of work are the city coun-

cil's instant headache, which, apart from islands' innate mistrust of the mainland, makes
for a poor reception of the latter's blueprints,
however breathtaking. Appealing as they may
be elsewhere, promises of universal employ-
ment and growth make little sense in a city
barely eight miles in circumference, which
even at the apogee of its maritime fortunes
never exceeded 200,000 souls. Such prospects
may thrill a shopkeeper or perhaps a doctor; a
mortician, though, would object, since the local cemeteries are jammed as it is and the dead
now should be buried on the mainland. In the
final analysis, that's what the mainland is good
for.

Still, had the mortician and the doctor belonged to different political parties, that would
be fine, some progress could be made. In this
city, they often belong to the same, and things
get stalled rather early, even if the party is the
PCI. In short, underneath all these squabbles,
unwitting ones or otherwise, lies the simple
truth that islands don't grow. That's what

money, a.k.a. the future, a.k.a. voluble politicos and fat cats, can't take, fails to grasp. What's worse, it feels defied by this place, since beauty, a *fait accompli* by definition, always defies the future, regarding it as nothing so much as an overblown, impotent present, or as its fading ground. If this place is reality (or, as some claim, the past), then the future with all its aliases is excluded from it. At best, it amounts to the present. And perhaps nothing proves this better than modern art, whose poverty alone makes it prophetic. A poor man always speaks for the present, and perhaps the sole function of collections like Peggy Guggenheim's and the similar accretions of this century's stuff habitually mounted here is to show what a cheap, self-assertive, ungenerous, one-dimensional lot we have become, to instill humility in us: there is no other outcome thinkable against the background of this Penelope of a city, weaving her patterns by day and undoing them by night, with no Ulysses in sight. Only the sea.

think it was Hazlitt who said that the only thing that could beat this city of water would be a city built in the air. That was a Calvinoesque idea, and who knows, as an upshot of space travel, that may yet come to pass. As it is, apart from the moon landing, this century may be best remembered by leaving this place intact, by just letting it be. I, for one, would advise even against gentle interference. Of course, film festivals and book fairs are in tune with the flickering of the canals' surface, with their curlicue, sirocco-perused scribblings. And of course, turning this place into a capital of scientific research would be a palatable option, especially taking into account the likely advantages of the local phosphorus-rich diet for any mental endeavor. The same bait could be used for moving the EEC headquarters here from Brussels and the European parliament from Strasbourg. And of course, a better solution would be to give this city and some of its environs the status of a national

park. Yet I would argue that the idea of turning Venice into a museum is as absurd as the urge to revitalize it with new blood. For one thing, what passes for new blood is always in the end plain old urine. And secondly, this city doesn't qualify to be a museum, being itself a work of art, the greatest masterpiece our species produced. You don't revive a painting, let alone a statue. You leave them alone, you guard them against vandals—whose hordes may include yourself.

easons are metaphors for available continents, and winter is always somewhat ant-arctic, even here. The city doesn't rely on coal as much as it used to; now it's gas. The magnificent, trumpetlike chimneys resembling medieval turrets in the back-drop of every Madonna and Crucifixion idle and gradually crumble away from the local

skyline. As a result you shiver and go to bed with your woolen socks on, because radiators keep their erratic cycles here even in hotels. Only alcohol can absorb the polar lightning shooting through your body as you set your foot on the marble floor, slippers or no slippers, shoes or no shoes. If you work in the evening you burn parthenons of candles—not for ambience or better light, but for their illusory warmth; or else you move to the kitchen, light the gas stove, and shut the door. Everything emanates cold, the walls especially. Windows you don't mind because you know what to expect from them. In fact, they only pass the cold through, whereas walls store it. I remember once spending the month of January in an apartment on the fifth floor of a house near the church of Fava. The place belonged to a descendant of none other than Ugo Foscolo. The owner was a forest engineer or some such thing, and was, naturally, away on business. The apartment wasn't that big: two rooms, sparsely furnished. The ceiling, though, was extraordinarily high and the windows were correspondingly tall. There were six or seven of them, as the apartment was a corner one. In the middle of the second week the heating went off. This time I was not alone, and my comrade-in-arms and I drew lots as to who would have to sleep by the wall. "Why should I always go to the wall?" she'd ask beforehand. "Because I'm a victim?" And her mustard-and-honey eyes would darken with incredulity upon losing. She would bundle up for the night—pink woolen jersey, scarf, stockings, long socks—and, having counted *uno, due, tre!* jump into the bed as though it were a dark river. To her, an Italian, a Roman, with a dash of Greek blood in her veins, it probably was. "The only thing I disagree with in Dante," she used to remark, "is the way he describes Hell. To me, Hell is cold, very cold. I'd keep the circles but make them of ice, with the temperature dropping with every spiral.

Hell is the Arctic." She meant it, too. With the scarf around her neck and head she looked like Francesco Querini on that statue in the Giardini, or like the famous bust of Petrarch (who, in turn, to me is the very image of Montale—or, rather, vice versa). There was no telephone in that place; a jumble of tuba-like chimneys loomed in the dark sky. The whole thing felt like the Flight to Egypt, with her playing both the woman and the child, and me my namesake and the donkey; after all, it was January. "Between Herod of the past and Pharaoh of the future," I kept telling myself. "Between Herod and Pharaoh, that's where we are." In the end I fell ill. Cold and dampness got me—or rather my chest muscles and nerves, messed up by surgeries. The cardiac cripple in me panicked and she somehow shoved me onto the train for Paris, as we both were unsure of the local hospitals, much though I adore the façade of Giovanni e Paolo. The carriage was warm, my head was splitting from nitro pills, a bunch of *bersaglieri* in the compartment were celebrating their home leave with Chianti and a ghetto blaster. I wasn't sure whether I would make it to Paris; but what was interfering with my fear was the clear sense that, should I manage, in no time at all—well, in a year—I'd be back to the cold place between Herod and Pharaoh. Even then, huddling on the wooden bench of my compartment, I was fully aware of this feeling's absurdity; yet as long as it could help me to see through my fear, absurdity was welcome. The trundling of the carriage and the effect of its constant vibration on one's frame did, I suppose, the rest, rearranging or messing up my muscles, etc., even further. Or maybe it was just that the heating in the carriage worked. At any rate, I made Paris, had a passable EKG, and boarded my plane for the States. In other words, lived to tell the story, and the story itself to repeat.

taly," Anna Akhmatova used to say, "is a dream that keeps returning for the rest of your life." It must be noted, though, that the arrival of dreams is irregular and their interpretation is yawn-inspiring. Furthermore, should dreams ever be designated a genre, their main stylistic device would doubtless be the non sequitur. That at least could be a justification for what has transpired thus far in these pages. Also, that could explain my attempts over all these years to secure that dream's recurrence, manhandling my superego in the process no less savagely than my unconscious. To put it bluntly, I kept returning myself to the dream, rather than the other way around. Sure enough, somewhere along the line I had to pay for this sort of violence, either by eroding what constituted my reality or by forcing the dream to acquire mortal features, the way the soul does in the course of one's lifetime. I guess I paid in both ways; and I didn't mind

it either, especially the latter, which would take the form of a *Cartavenezia* (exp. date, Jan. 1988) in my wallet, anger in those eyes of a particular variety (trained, and as of the same date, on better sights), or something equally finite. The reality suffered more, and often I would be crossing the Atlantic on my way home with a distinct feeling of traveling from history into anthropology. For all the time, blood, ink, money, and the rest that I shed or shelled out here, I never could convincingly claim, even to myself, that I'd acquired any local traits, that I'd become, in however minuscule a manner, a Venetian. A vague smile of recognition on the face of a hotelier or a trattoria proprietor didn't count; nor could anyone be deceived by the clothes I'd purchased locally. Gradually, I've become a transient in either realm, with the failure of convincing the dream of my presence in it being somewhat more disheartening. That, of course, was familiar. Yet I suppose a case could be made for fidelity when one returns to the place of one's love, year after year, in the wrong season, with no guarantee of being loved back. For, like every virtue, fidelity is of value only so long as it is instinctive or idiosyncratic, rather than rational. Besides, at a certain age, and in a certain line of work at that, to be loved back is not exactly imperative. Love is a selfless sentiment, a one-way street. That's why it is possible to love cities, architecture per se, music, dead poets, or, given a particular temperament, a deity. For love is an affair between a reflection and its object. This is in the end what brings one back to this city—the way the tide brings the Adriatic and, by extension, the Atlantic and the Baltic. At any rate, objects don't ask questions: as long as the element exists, their reflection is guaranteed—in the form of a returning traveler or in the form of a dream, for a dream is the fidelity of the shut eye. That's the sort of confidence our own kind is lacking, although we are part water.

hould the world be designated a genre, its main stylistic device would no doubt be water. If that doesn't happen, it is either because the Almighty, too, doesn't seem to have much in the way of alternatives, or because a thought itself possesses a water pattern. So does one's handwriting; so do one's emotions; so does blood. Reflection is the property of liquid substances, and even on a rainy day one can always prove the superiority of one's fidelity to that of glass by positioning oneself behind it. This city takes one's breath away in every weather, the variety of which, at any rate, is somewhat limited. And if we are indeed partly synonymous with water, which is fully synonymous with time, then one's sentiment toward this place improves the future, contributes to that Adriatic or Atlantic of time which stores our reflections for when we are long gone. Out of them, as out of frayed sepia pictures, time will perhaps be able to fashion, in a collage-like manner, a version of the future

better than it would be without them. This way one is a Venetian by definition, because out there, in its equivalent of the Adriatic or Atlantic or Baltic, time-alias-water crochets or weaves our reflections—alias love for this place—into unrepeatable patterns, much like the withered old women dressed in black all over this littoral's islands, forever absorbed in their eye-wrecking lacework. Admittedly, they go blind or mad before they reach the age of fifty, but then they get replaced by their daughters and nieces. Among fishermen's wives, the Parcae never have to advertise for an opening.

he one thing the locals never do is ride gondolas. To begin with, a gondola ride is pricey. Only foreign tourists, and well-off ones at that, can afford it. That's what explains the median age of gondola passengers: a septuagenarian can shell out one-tenth of a

schoolteacher's salary without wincing. The sight of these decrepit Romeos and their rickety Juliets is invariably sad and embarrassing, not to say ghastly. For the young, i.e., for those for whom this sort of thing would be appropriate, a gondola is as far out of reach as a five-star hotel. Economy, of course, reflects demography; yet that is doubly sad, because beauty, instead of promising the world, gets reduced to being its reward. That, in parenthesis, is what drives the young to nature, whose free, or, more exactly, cheap delights are free—i.e., devoid—of the meaning and invention present in art or in artifice. A landscape can be thrilling, but a façade by Lombardini tells you what you can do. And one way—the original way—of looking at such façades is from a gondola: this way you can see what the water sees. Of course, nothing could be further from the locals' agendas as they scurry and bustle about on their daily rounds, properly oblivious or even allergic to the surrounding splendor. The closest they come to using a gondola is when they're ferried across the Grand Canal or carrying home some unwieldy purchase—a washing machine, say, or a sofa. But neither a ferryman nor a boat owner would on such occasions break into "*O sole mio*." Perhaps the indifference of a native takes its cue from artifice's own indifference to its own reflection. That could be the locals' final argument against the gondola, except that it could be countered by the offer of a ride at nighttime, to which I once succumbed.

The night was cold, moonlit, and quiet. There were five of us in the gondola, including its owner, a local engineer who, together with his girlfriend, did all the paddling. We moseyed and zigzagged like an eel through the silent town hanging over our heads, cavernous and empty, resembling at this late hour a vast, largely rectangular coral reef or a succession of uninhabited grottoes. It was a peculiar sensation: to find yourself moving within what you're used to glancing across—canals; it felt like acquiring an extra dimension. Presently we glided into the *laguna* and headed toward the island of the dead, toward San Michele. The moon, pitched extraordinarily high, like some mind-bogglingly sharp ti crossed by a cloud's ledger sign, was barely available to the sheet of water, and the gondola's gliding too was absolutely noiseless. In fact, there was something distinctly erotic in the noiseless and traceless passage of its lithe body upon the water—much like sliding your palm down the smooth skin of your beloved. Erotic, because there were no consequences, because the skin was infinite and almost immobile, because the caress was abstract. With us inside, the gondola was perhaps slightly heavy, and the water momentarily yielded underneath, only to close the gap the very next second. Also, powered by a man and a woman, the gondola wasn't even masculine. In fact, it was an eroticism not of genders but of elements, a perfect match of their equally lacquered surfaces. The sensation was neutral, almost incestuous, as though you were present as a brother caressed his sister, or vice versa. In this manner we circled the island of the dead and headed back to Canareggio . . . Churches, I always thought, should stay open all night; at least the Madonna dell' Orto should—not so much because of the likely timing of the soul's agony as because of the wonderful Bellini *Madonna with Child* in it. I wanted to disembark there and steal a glance at the painting, at the inch-wide interval that separates her left palm from the Child's sole. That inch—ah, much less!—is what separates love from eroticism. Or perhaps that's the ultimate in eroticism. But the cathedral was closed and we proceeded through the tunnel of grottoes, through this abandoned, flat, moonlit Piranesian mine with its few sparkles of electric ore, to the heart of the city. Still, now I knew what water feels like being caressed by water.

e disembarked near the concrete crate of the Bauer Grünwald Hotel, rebuilt after the war, toward the end of which it was blown up by the local partisans because it housed the German command. As an eyesore, it keeps good company with the church of San Moisè—the busiest façade in town. Together, they look like Albert Speer having a pizza *capricciosa*. I've never been inside either, but I knew a German gentleman who stayed in this crate-like structure and found it very comfortable. His mother was dying while he was on vacation here and he spoke to her daily over the telephone. When she expired he convinced the management to sell him the telephone's receiver. The management understood, and the receiver was included in the bill. But then he was most likely a Protestant, while San Moisè is a Catholic church, not to mention its being closed at night.

quidistant from our respective abodes, this was as good a place to disembark as any. It takes about an hour to cross this city by foot in any direction. Provided, of course, that you know your way, which by the time I stepped out of that gondola I did. We bade each other farewell and dispersed. I walked toward my hotel, tired, not even trying to look around, mumbling to myself some odd, God-knows-from-where-dredged-up lines, like "Pillage this village," or "This city deserves no pity." That sounded like early Auden, but it wasn't. Suddenly I wanted a drink. I swerved into San Marco in the hope that Florian's was still open. It was closing; they were removing the chairs from the arcade and mounting wooden boards on the windows. A short negotiation with the waiter, who had already changed to go home but whom I knew slightly, had the desired result; and with that result in hand I stepped out from

under the arcade and scanned the piazza. It was absolutely empty, not a soul. Its four hundred rounded windows were running in their usual maddening order, like idealized waves. This sight always reminded me of the Roman Colosseum, where, in the words of a friend of mine, somebody invented the arch and couldn't stop. "Pillage this village," I was still muttering to myself. "This city deserves . . ." Fog began to engulf the piazza. It was a quiet invasion, but an invasion nonetheless. I saw its spears and lances moving silently but very fast, from the direction of the *laguna*, like foot soldiers preceding their heavy cavalry. "Silently, and very fast," I said to myself. Any time now you could anticipate their king, King Fog, appearing from around the corner in all his cumulus glory. "Silently, and very fast," I repeated to myself. Now, that was Auden's last line from his "Fall of Rome," and it was this place that was "altogether elsewhere." All of a sudden I felt he was behind me, and I turned as fast as I could. A tall, smooth window of Florian's that was reasonably well lit and not covered with a board gleamed through the patches of fog. I walked toward it and looked inside. Inside, it was 195?. On the red plush divans, around a small marbled table with a kremlin of drinks and teapots on it, sat Wystan Auden, with his great love, Chester Kallman, Cecil Day Lewis and his wife, Stephen Spender and his. Wystan was telling some funny story and everybody was laughing. In the middle of the story, a well-built sailor passed by the window; Chester got up and, without so much as a "See you later," went in hot pursuit. "I looked at Wystan," Stephen told me years later. "He kept laughing, but a tear ran down his cheek." At this point, for me, the window had gone dark. King Fog rode into the piazza, reined in his stallion, and started to unfurl his white turban. His buskins were wet, so was his charivari; his cloak was studded with the dim, myopic jewels of burning lamps. He was dressed that way because he hadn't any idea what century it was, let alone which year. But then, being fog, how could he?

et me reiterate: Water equals time and provides beauty with its double. Part water, we serve beauty in the same fashion. By rubbing water, this city improves time's looks, beautifies the future. That's what the role of this city in the universe is. Because the city is static while we are moving. The tear is proof of that. Because we go and beauty stays. Because we are headed for the future, while beauty is the eternal present. The tear is an attempt to remain, to stay behind, to merge with the city. But that's against the rules. The tear is a throwback, a tribute of the future to the past. Or else it is the result of subtracting the greater from the

lesser: beauty from man. The same goes for love, because one's love, too, is greater than oneself.

November 1989